PINK TREES PRESS

Not since Chelsey Minnis's *Baby, I Don't Care* has poetry been this much fun: "You kiss me so hard I want a restraining order. / Kiss me harder." This New York: "The worst thing about living / in a doorman building / is that you have to pass the doorman / every day." This noir: "What do I know about life anyway? / Except how fast a cigarette can burn / next to a cocktail / when the money isn't mine." This philosophical: "love is the taxi I'll never find in a downpour." *Night of the Manhattans* is a julep of a book ... and a Manhattan. You'll want to order another.

—Tim Tomlinson, author of *Listening to Fish: Meditations from the Wet World.*

Juneau's poetry takes us to those late-night places alive in our gut. Boozy nights. A woman caught between love and a drink. There's so much want. Be it afternoon or after midnight. This masterfully crafted collection insists upon being devoured. Read it late at night in one sitting, then read it again. A book you won't want to put down.

— Nicca Ray, author of the memoir *Ray by Ray: A Daughter's Take on the Legend of Nicholas Ray*, and poetry collections, *Backseat Baby, Curve,* and *Go Go Go Girl.*

Juneau's compelling and insightful poetry guides the reader through a life experienced within the vibrant and ceaseless energy of New York City. In *Night of the Manhattans,* every moment embraces the allure and chaos of urban life.

— Nancy Mercado, American Book Award for Lifetime Achievement

Night of the Manhattans

Titles from Pink Trees Press

Silver Tongued Devil Anthology,
Linda Kleinbub & Anthony C. Murphy, Editors
Poems from an Unending Pandemic, Phillip Giambri
Dysfunction: A Play on Words in the Familiar, Pauline Findlay
Good Boy, Bad Boy, A Better Man, Phillip Giambri
Naming a Hurricane, Madeline Artenberg
The Bookstore Book, Ron Kolm
Spellbook of Ordinary Mistakes, Jane LeCroy
Appear to Dance, Linda Kleinbub
Night of the Manhattans, Jennifer Juneau

For more information:
pinktreespress@gmail.com

Night of the Manhattans

Poems

Jennifer Juneau

Pink Trees Press
New York City

Cover Art: Linda Wulkan
Author Photo: Linda Kleinbub

Published in the United States of America by
Pink Trees Press, Inc.
Middle Village, NY 11379

First Edition: June 2025
ISBN: 979-8-9898695-9-6
Library of Congress Control Number:
2025940104

Acknowledgments

Many thanks to all the editors who published these poems in the following journals, sometimes in slightly different form. I am truly grateful:

Barrow Street: "Last Call"
Boog City Arts Festival 2025: "Nueva Primavera"
Brownstone Poets Anthology: "After a Late Night Jazz Event on the Outskirts of Brooklyn" and "Good Luck Coffee, or, Why Can't I Find Subject Matter for Poems Like I Used to?"
Café Review: "In Some Café on the Upper West Side" and "Who Hasn't"
Gargoyle Magazine: "Doorman Building," "Fuck You, Jennifer: A Love Poem," and "You Told Me, Y, to Write You a Love Poem"
Live Mag!: "I Slept with Jay Last Night"
Local Knowledge Magazine: "Night of the Manhattans"
The Long-Islander: "Electric" and "Pipe Dream"
Meat For Tea: "Grub Hub Rant," "I'm Mad About a Lot of Things Prayer," "No, You Didn't Miss My Reading," and "On Essex Street"
Pine Hills Review: "What Isn't Love"
Poetry Bay: "Lunch with Girlfriends" and "One True Thing"
Rattle: "For the Girl Crying on the Steps"
Sensitive Skin Magazine: "A Kind of Love Story," "Something Good is Going to Happen Today" and "There is No Brooklyn Bound F Service"
Soup Can Magazine: "I Wish February Would Never End"
South Florida Poetry Journal: "Big Lee's" and "I Bet You Don't Look at the Skyline Like You Used To"

Suitcase of Chrysanthemums (Great Weather for Media): "A Secret Between You and Me"
Treehouse: "Somewhere Near the Bowery"

"A Kind of Love Story" was reprinted in *NYC From the Inside* (Blue Light Press) and *Sensitive Skin Anthology Selected Writing: 2016-2018*

"Grub Hub Rant" received Honorable Mention for *Great Weather for Media's Poem of the Week* online

"Lunch with Girlfriends" received a Readers' Choice Award for poetry published in *Poetry Bay's Poems and Illuminations*

Table of Contents

For Mas Walker
and all my friends from A to Z
on the New York City Poetry Scene

Night of the Manhattans

Times Square

Its giddy billboards make me dizzy,
glitzy and lit like the face of a tourist.
This is not my New York—
it's owned by Disney.
Give me the lusty filth of Taxi Driver;
let a real rain wash away the comic relief.
Give me xxx movies early a.m. maybe 2 or 3.
I want to see one with Joe Buck
from Midnight Cowboy.
Peep shows in theaters dim
with muted reds and pinks.
Hookers in short shorts on 42nd Street
swinging their purse strings
like nobody's business. Give me the danger
of Port Authority late night.
Give me the jazz of midtown.
24-hour diners on 10th.
Strangers in dive bars on 8th and 9th.
Don't follow me with your overzealous smile,
Mickey, and high-pitched mouse voice.
That ain't real life.

Electric

It's your eyes that nearly kill me
when they burn straight into mine.
Follow me to the basement of $5.00 margaritas.
Follow me drunk $15.00 later up to the band
and watch me ask the bass player
if he has a girlfriend.
Just to make you jealous.
So that we can create the flames
that make poetry happen.
So that we can create the throbbing of a song.
Because every bed needs hands and fingers.
The ceiling is falling with illumination.
I have never held the gaze of a man this long
without making an entire room disappear.
Get into me, intimate as that poem
or that song that can burn down a nation.
Impulse is pulsating at the door,
let's get out of here,
because spontaneity can't be planned.
Remember, only idiots fall vacant at the tongue
(we won't be one of them.)
This has nothing to do with speaking.

Crackpot

Do you want to go out for a drink?
Do you even drink?
I'll wear my hair long.
Maybe I'll wear it up.
Or pull it back.
We can spoil ourselves on plum wine
and Chinatown clams.
I don't eat clams, but who cares!
The night is like a glistening form of carbon.
Watch what you say when you're feeling
you know, moody
and lovey all at once.
You can send the text,
but you can't take it back.
You are at risk for a [broken] heart-attack.
I'll just stand over there, pretend I'm not here.
Make sure when things are good
not to pick up your phone.
Let the silence remind you
why you're sitting alone.

A Secret Between You and Me

Finding a lover is like finding a job.
The good ones are taken.
The bad ones are temporary.
It's like finding the life you have lived
from time to time to time
on late-night streets ruined with erroneous
weather. So I guess not all hope is lost.
But what I'd like to know is:
Who invented mirrors?
"Love makes everything wrong."
"Love breaks everyone's heart."
"We're here to ruin ourselves."
"We're here to love the wrong people."
Every night I pray to a god I don't believe in
and ask him, or her, or it,
to help me love the wrong person,
to help me ruin myself,
to help me to *wrong* the right *everything*
so when the day comes
when I'm so so wrong it isn't funny
it suddenly feels right.
I can tell myself this, that I've gotten away
with something big.
I've solved life's greatest mystery, and well,
now I'm a hero.

This has nothing to do with how loud the horn
blazes midnight through a tunnel.
It's the tequila-drenched version of myself
that calls the shots.
The stale remnants of musical notes throb
inside my head, then dissolve like a boozy
afterthought, like a wizened hooker
at the end of her heyday who turns tricks
cheap, cheaper for murderous men.
Reminding me that it isn't my life
and the music wasn't all that good.
What do I know about life anyway?
Except how fast a cigarette can burn
next to a cocktail
when the money isn't mine.

I Bet You Don't Look at the Skyline Like You Used To

How much change can you spare?
Do you want your windshield washed?
In fact, I'd rather walk
because you don't own a car.
Why seven-layer cake?
Because no beggar begs for fruit.
Enough of the small talk.
We pour into a bar.
Here comes another shot.
With juice, maybe not, but
I like my vodka straight.
You drink yours straight, too.
The walls go from sodium to blue.
In a tight space the crowd melts away.
We see each other through vodka eyes.
The crowd refills the room.
The band does its thing.
I sway to the hypnotic strings of bass.
As if this city never happened,
outside voices fade.
I turn my want of you away
and put it in another time and place.

What Isn't Love

Since you ask, love, that's not a question.
Love isn't haggled at a flea market
like a brass lamp. You can't money me for love
like a honey-dipped coat.
Love isn't hanging out festively
on East 10th Street
when the mood is wrecked by bygones
and has-beens. What isn't love
is between the sheets of rain
without the definition of weather.
Love isn't your touchdowns, your rice and beans,
your spoils of war.
Love isn't your west side story.
Love isn't love when the bottle is empty
but nobody's drunk. Because
what isn't love is nobody's red sock
and somebody's black boot. What isn't love
is everyone's pair of glasses that ruins the view.
What isn't love is when the bread rots
because someone forgot to check
the last sale date. Love isn't love
when the number's been blocked.
What isn't love, you ask? That's not a question.
Love isn't love when the horn sounds
but the brakes forget to stop. What isn't love
is because what isn't love is not.

In Some Café on the Upper West Side

she said she'd never sleep with a man
she'd known less than six months
she's afraid she'll bruise the virgin mary, she said
& all she'd been taught in a plaid skirt;
it wouldn't be smart to talk about first dates,
i thought, or the fact that life's too short
so i ordered a dirty martini
she drank holy water from a paper cup
who hasn't died of ecstasy one time or another
you know what i'm talking about i hope

later the sun broke through clouds
and i took the F train to the lower east side
she hopped a taxi to her flight at jfk
(or maybe to newark i wasn't sure)
back to the west coast
i thought of van gogh and what he once said:
something about dying of passion
& i'd rather & boredom
and i assembled a poem & sent it to myself by
text and read it on stage to a lively crowd
in a dim & happening place

Big Lee's

On a late night, walking my coffee cup,
I headed to buy cough drops close to the theatre.
Instead, I found myself in Big Lee's
on 1st Avenue ordering tequila.
A voice said, Make mine a double.
(I swear I didn't say it, ask the bartender.)
(Who happened to be blonde and buxom.)
She was putting on lipstick.
I was having a bad hair day.
Two men shot pool.
A man next to me at the bar was speaking
into his whisky glass.
Can I bum a cigarette? I asked.
Then I asked: Who is Big Lee?
He said, A neon-lit sign, loopy and red.
He said, You lose a bit of god with each sip.
There's truth in those sips,
you just need to know where to look.
The stars are aligned, so what.
I cracked a blanket in half by the river.
I thought I'd find you on train tracks
but you were caught in a blizzard
in the middle of Spring.

Night of the Manhattans

We went to A's book launch at KGB Bar
and B bought a round of manhattans
then C bought a round of manhattans
with extra cherries
then I bought a round of champagne
and we drank and we drank and we drank
(you'd think we never drank before.)
C had too much champagne
and said she thought she was going to puke
because she can't mix
and B told us a hilarious joke
someone from the front
told us to shut up in the back. A wasn't upset
because she was killing it on stage with the most
amazing poem
it was so good I videotaped it
flash bulbs went off in all directions
so B made another joke
that nobody else could hear
which sent me to the floor dying.
Then B left early because she had other plans,
she always had other plans.
C and I got drunk(er)
we went around kissing (every)(one).
We kissed D.
We kissed E,

F & G.
And D made a joke about A taking C and me
away from her,
and I said it was her right because after all
it was her book launch.
And C flew to Paris shortly after that
and I was left, just me and my manhattans
(with that flute of champagne in between)
and no cherry.

A Kind of Love Story

Walking along Avenue A, I was kind of drunk.
It was kind of desolate and kind of late.
All the stores were kind of closed
and there was this guy
who kind of looked like you.
He kind of smiled.
I kind of smiled too.
He kind of waved me over.

I kind of went to him whatever.
He kind of smoked a cigarette.
He kind of put his arm around me
and I kind of let him.
We kind of walked over to his place.

He kind of had me alone.
He kind of showed me his record collection
and we kind of listened to old jazz,
the Rolling Stones.
He kind of lit a blunt.
We kind of smoked it.

He kind of had a bottle of Tennessee whiskey.
Well, you can guess what we kind of did with that.
We kind of kissed in the half shadow moonlight.
Then we kind of did other things, kind of.

In the morning, he said he kind of wanted
to take me on a long car trip.
I said I was kind of down with that.
I kind of felt I was in love.
He said he kind of felt it too.

We kind of packed up everything he owned
and skipped town.
This, because you stood me up.
That was very kind of kind of you.

I Slept with Jay Last Night

Because life.
Because all those death poems.
And eleni.
And all the world's lovers.
And the XYZ pub was dark that night,
all those ailments and complaints.
Which made sasha upset.
Which made eleni upset.
Which made me upset.
And sasha needs to rearrange her chapbook.
And eleni's having nightmares of abuse and death.
And eleni wouldn't read her metaphysical poem
with Greece in her voice.
And I'm still young.
And I'm still pretty.
So I slept with jay last night.
The XYZ reading was depressing,
all those ailments and words of death.
Eleni's breasts were put on trial.
And sasha was upset.
And eleni was upset.
And I was upset.
And sasha left early.
And eleni went home with nightmares.
And jay   was waiting
                              full of life.

Somewhere Near the Bowery

2 a.m. and it's so cold out
my face is about to fall off.
I empty pennies into the hand of a drifter.
Humans will evolve into mythological creatures,
he yells after me.
E walks home, taking her accent with her.
A swan, with one gold eye,
smack in the middle of New York City
follows me to the 24-hour Rite Aid
for a Kit Kat and a Coke.
To the Second Avenue subway.
To the last drag of a cigarette before it's out.
Your name in lights.
(Jesus, it's cold.)
(But there's nothing he could do.)
The weather is planning us:
Let's solve it together.

Last Call

Mr. Cream Pop
follow my stockings
home. Pour me a drink as derelict
as the panic on the rec room rug. Chase me
into the kitchen after I stomp out in a hissy fit.
Like he always did. That's phony, you said.
That's what people in movies did
or how your past lovers tread.
Fix me leftover pizza
with burrata and cherry tomatoes.
Heat it till it burns like the last star
will disappear into the crepuscular light.
You wouldn't be caught dead
in a tangle of fishnets
because who is married? But not tonight.
Come to my rescue
with a cigarette and an accent.
I like your watch. Stay a little longer
if only one night.

Tripwire

I want you bad and would rather be dead.
There's laughter in the hallway
outside my studio door. The workmen
are walking up the stairs. Soon
they will hammer and drill
into something in the vacant apartment above.
I think, as the light fixture next to the tub shakes,
one of the workers will fall through the ceiling.
A welcomed distraction from you and death.
I won't take a bath,
I'm not in the mood to get covered
with insalubrious dust. Instead
I go upstairs to see what's up. I ask
the workmen if they'll fall through my ceiling,
sounds that way, feels that way
and one of them smiles and says, "Ok."
The other worker waves his arms and says, "No,
no." Says, "Don't worry. We break, we pay."
Things break all the time. They stay broken
and nobody cares to fix them. Nobody pays.
Even if the words come with a different face.

Grub Hub Rant

After placing my food order
instead of one bag of chips and a Diet Coke
I see I ordered two bags of chips by accident
so I call the restaurant
and the chef says, yes Jennifer, I see your order
and, yes Jennifer, one bag of chips
one Coke no problem
and I correct him, 'Diet Coke' because, you know,
along with the fried schnitzel and the chips
you need Diet Coke as if it matters.
And it matters.
He hems and haws.

I bet he's thinking that I'm thinking
it's the end of the world if my order is wrong
and it is
the end of the world sometimes.
And it is the end of the world in my nighttime
glitches of pandemics and police brutality
and stupid poems about food

and I find myself getting all made up
for the delivery guy because, where else do I go?
I sit in my West Village studio all day
and moan and sometimes write
about, about, about Grub Hub orders being wrong

and so expensive, I mean expansive,
and my phone suddenly rings.
It's the chef this time he's calling me asking me
what kind of chips I wanted:
sour cream, salt & vinegar, salt & pepper, cheddar
and—and I stop him right there and say
salt & pepper and he says with the Coke?
And I correct him, 'Diet Coke' as if it matters.
And it matters
and he's says very good
and I'm thinking he's thinking he had to call me
back to check because it feels like
the end of the world if I got the wrong chips
and this time I think that he seriously thinks
it is the end of the world and it is, sometimes
and it feels so good, so, so good
that we're all in this together.

The Novel I Never Wrote

The novel I never wrote unfolds in my head.
The one that haunts me but will never be read.
The novel that is never coming out.
The novel I told all of my friends about.
The novel that swallowed ten chapters whole.
The novel with a dozen main characters, all true.
The novel born in New Jersey.
The novel analyzing my fear of empty spaces.
The novel a flourishing oak in suburbia.
The novel that's never hungry.
The novel that popped the raw ripe flesh
between my legs.
The novel that gets me stoned.
The novel that follows me to Boston
gets me drunk and takes me home.
The novel that takes my hand in marriage
on a beach in Puerto Rico.
The novel I cook for.
The novel I raise.
The novel that puts me on a plane.
The novel in German translation.
The novel that continues to fuck me
while I dream about the novel I want to fuck.
The prescription painkiller novel.
The New York City novel.

The novel that exhausts and will someday kill me.
The novel I will die for
without ever having touched.

Fuck You, Jennifer: A Love Poem

-After an email from an editor, because we, as a
nation, can say anything we want

Fuck you, Jennifer, fuck you.
Fuck you and your shitty poems.
Fuck you and your crappy novel.
You selfish bitch.
All you want is to be famous.
Go fuck Jack.
(I have no idea who Jack is.)
Go fuck Jack hard.
(Sounds like Dr. Seuss.)
Fuck you.
You fucked yourself with XYZ Press and every
fucking person I know.
I want nothing to do with your crappy work.
Fuck you Jennifer, fuck you. You are stupid.
(Man, I love this email so much
I want to jerk it off.)
Fuck you. You are a piece of work.
You are a therapist's dream.
Fuck you. Fuck you.

65 Morton Street

I've misplaced time.
I look for you in a faded afternoon
sewn into daylight savings. When
the light wanes from the Earth's outline

I look for you in a faded afternoon
while engaged in prayer. Late to bed
the light waned from the Earth's outline
my body is half awake.

Engaged in prayer and late to bed
I search for six months ago
half awake
in the pocket of a clock set back.

I search for six months ago
in the dense grove of your lifetime
in the pocket of a clock set back
with thoughts of seeing you again.

In the dense grove of your lifetime
sewn into daylight savings
thoughts of seeing you again
misplace time.

Lunch with Girlfriends

We talk about fate
and the good it brings
like passengers whose lives were saved
because they didn't board a doomed plane
or a miscarriage being nature's way
of sparing us later pain.
Serious stuff.
Like the time I didn't go see X's band play
and S noted that it was a good thing
because I hadn't lost the weight yet
and how strange, come to think of it,
I couldn't get any of my friends
to go with me that night as if they knew.
E stepped in
and reminded me that I hadn't gotten my roots
dyed yet either.
Keep on talking, girls.
Now he's with someone else, I know this,
so I suppose it would do no good to say
I'm different now, find me,
I'm smarter, thinner
and in a better place.
Make no mistake
my friends and I believe

that we are the best thing
to ever happen to a room.
But there are a million of us
and we don't always aim to please
but to think what didn't end up as a killer fling
and why we torture ourselves
by pining for what is capable of breaking us,
why can't I say this right,
this is not a question, don't stop me,
why can't I say I never wanted to be in love
with a sure thing? What I'm saying is:
It's the way he looked at her.
The way he'll never look at me.

On Essex Street

I walk past *Wholesome Foods* and I'm thinking
there's nothing wholesome about this place
it's just how I like it.
The old linoleum floors reek
of my youth in all its filth & beauty
& it's 100 degrees out.
Next door a crowded bar with its door wide open
and its ceiling fan spinning like a record
on a turntable lures me in.
The stale scent of barley & hops
is worn into the wood.
One bottle of cold Miller later
I'm back on the spit-filled & cracked concrete.
The air is not ablaze with colors, no shooting
stars, no quixotic lens I walk through
just achromatic, bare-naked humidity,
this summer's day with no breeze.
And I got this, I got this fusion of the senses.
Don't fall in love, I tell myself.
This feeling has no name, only a consequence.
If I could toss all those wasted lovers
of the past away, the ones that failed
and the ones that didn't
I'd exchange every fraction of bliss that had fallen
and risen for this one.
I've seen him up there

belting out one love song after the next
with that body language
and that voice
evenly measured like drops of honey.
Here's the thing:
I don't know how to play this.
Here's another thing:
Yes, I do.
Or, the thing is
there's no time to play this
whether you know how to or not.
I'm dizzy with all this drizzle waiting to erupt
like the atmosphere stricken
with the wrong weather.
I don't want to fall
and I don't want to fall
but falling keeps forcing its way through.
I'm spent on the energy
it takes to want someone this bad.
Then this:
Proximity.
How close you come after the sound of the last
guitar string strummed falls dead.
The silence is strung-out in echoes
and the notes fall away as they settle in thin air

and the end of motion leaves this vision
in stillness, leaving this pursuit to be sealed
into another chapter of wanting.

East Village House Party

You had to have it on the coldest day of the year.
L, M, S & T couldn't be bothered to carry
all that beer onto the subway;
you took it personally.
J baked magic brownies,
P ate as many as he was able
and drank all the Jack Daniel's D brought,
the bottle disappearing from the table.

P insisted on sleeping over,
as he walked into a wall.
You fought him off your couch after he puked
all over the living room floor. I rebuked
you for not having a bucket near,
as our drunkest guest stumbled out the door.

The wine was tops, the cake and pizza went.
Despite the decorations and the money spent
next time, you remarked, you'll pack up
your ambient aspirations
and throw a party in the park.

No More Mr. Nice Guy

I'm sick of nice.
Give me a man who drinks hard liquor
like it's a life sentence.
One who smokes and does drugs.
A man who doesn't want to make love
but wants to fuck me like a selfish lover
over and over. Who doesn't care what I want.
Who will pull me towards him,
forcefully. Yank my hair.
Twist my blonde strands in his fist
until I'm lit with the fury of a rapturous god.
A man who will deny himself access to my face
so that I can be any one of his lovers.
To call me by another name.
To love me like a hot whiskey shot.
To love me with the pure sting of urinary fire.
Thankful friends, considerate men,
I'm sick of them. Give me a man
who will tear off my expensive silk with his teeth.
Swallow my rings.
One who will send me home in ripped fishnets.
Who won't call me to say I'm amazing, then flake
but who has the guts to say:
I can only commit to one-night stands.
I want a real man.

Someone who will leave every cell in my body
sick with longing I'll need to turn off my phone
so I won't hear him not calling me back.
No, no more Mr. Nice Guy
who will put my feet to sleep.
I need an honest man to keep me on my toes.
Not a man with a book of false promises
at the ready. Only liars have those.

Pipe Dream

In a Greenwich Village café, you materialized:
a living wannabe. We sat and chewed the fat
like we used to, while sipping

herbal tea. Wet-washed pedestrians flooded in
squandering our celestial rendezvous.

I became a dim-lit lump against a wall
envisioning the past inside my head
where you, among old lovers, tread.

That Guy

He's that kind of guy a girl would date
to get back at her parents.
He's a wild party you can't leave.
I wish the girl clacking her heels
in the hallway of my building
would shut up. Stop walking.
I can't hear myself think about that guy.
She's scaring the cats.
It's worse than the men in hard hats
outside my window drilling holes in the sidewalk
on Christopher Street.
Back to that guy.
That guy a girl would date
to get back at her parents.
That guy who calls once and awhile
and asks me to wear my loudest heels late
at night, to come clacking across his kitchen floor,
down the hall to his bedroom, clacking loud,
like some girl clacks in my hallway
when I'm alone and don't have that guy
a girl would date
but instead have only the men, in hard hats,
on Christopher Street
drilling holes in my concrete heart.

Cerveza Pacifico

Let's pretend we're in a beer commercial:
I, the girl with the long blonde hair
that glistens in the sun of your threadbare lamp.
My deep tan is a smudge of Revlon Cover Up,
my pink glossed lips
are sticky with jam. Let's make believe
as you step out of the shower thirsty for it,
your black hair dripping, that you'd just come
from the ocean, swollen and treacherous.
Your tongue curls like a wave inside my mouth
brackish with lime from your first sip. I dig
my nails into your back. I can't
escape the beachfront view wet with you
nor could my signature etched in sand.

Blank Blonde

We'll talk rocket science.
We'll put crackers on cheese.
We'll read books about chemistry.
What lurks underneath the swell of jealousy.
We'll criticize cigars and submarines.
Empty out the alarm bell of ugly props.
Oversleep in a creamy king bed.

The toast pops.
The eggshell cracks: pure gold flow.
Apply the bottle from the box.
Rinse and go.

Fringe Benefits

Call me so I can be mean to you.
I'm feeling
           awful-
ly passive-aggressive
           today.

The night showed up
           like a beer and a pickup truck,
so I come to you
   in silver cowboy boots,
a futuristic coat.

Your apartment is hayseedy. Smolders
in incense and herbs. Fruit flies, gnats.
           A condensed scent
between earthy and rank.

I waste your weed.
You kiss me so hard I want a restraining order.
           Kiss me harder.

We shove down tacos on 2nd Street
and Avenue A.
Midnight, I floss my teeth with razor blades.

My pain takes up too much space
        in the mirror!

But there's this tattoo I want to get, right here.
        It's got your name on it.

What does it mean to *want?*
What is *more*
        in Spanish?

One True Thing

I scrounge for change at the bottom of my purse.
You scrounge for change in your pockets.
We search the streets of the lower east side
for food at 1 a.m.
One plate of vegetarian curry.
One fork.
We stand at your kitchen table
and feed each other (you've expressed your
concern that I do not eat enough.)
I look around your east village walk-up:
One couch.
One bookcase-covered wall.
One big bed.
Your living room curtain is torn into art.
Cake icing is stuck to the wall, petrified.
I don't ask why
I imagine a heated argument.
Someone's lost temper.
A jealous ex-lover.
This turns me on.
There's a rabbit, there's a dog,
there's you & me in the moonlight
pouring over each other all night
like rain might come.
I count the rings on the ceiling while you sleep.
I count remote incandescent figures in the sky.

I don't find us starring in constellations
I find us at the bottom of an endless dream
I can't wake up from.
I reflect on a conversation I had with S & P.
I had given them heaps of expensive clothing
from my past life rich with the Rivieras of France
and Italy. S said she'd gladly stay
in a toxic marriage for all that.
I say she's crazy.
P is oblivious, as if she'd given up.
I'd given up once, too.
But sometimes you must give in
and harvest the benefits
gifted in all your lover's glory.
When you take him in your arms,
until you are ready to lose him.

You Told Me, Y, to Write You a Love Poem

but love has zero ambition after it's caught
love is dumb
deaf
& blind

love is the taxi I'll never find in a downpour
so that i'll get soaking wet with you
love is being intoxicated on the flowers
i never got
love is the heat of the bourbon shot i needed
to stomach the hurt
love is naming my longest strand of hair after you,
the one i won't cut

love is not having to write love on demand
when there are too many love poems
in the universe that mean shit

love   just   is
isn't that love poem enough?

No, You Didn't Miss My Reading

No, you didn't miss it. It's still on the 13th.
I was at another poet's reading.
I called because I thought you'd pop in
so I can see your lovely face.
Squeeze your hand under the table.
Corner you for a kiss when no one was looking.
Pretend we didn't know each other, what a thrill.
Slip back to your place,
have you in a moonlit room,
shiver while you turn me into honey,
tie your heart strings into double knots,
stumble out of your bed at the crack of dawn,
take forever to leave because,
although I have to leave
        I don't want to leave you.
Fumble with your door locks
(they've never been easy)
(or maybe I was willing them
to keep me locked in.)
Stop for a coffee around the corner
from the subway, write all day on zero sleep
and love it.
No, you didn't miss my reading.
I just missed you.

Drop Dead Gorgeous

You are one apple and a plate of spinach.
You are well-suited
well-skirted, and pant.
Well-stocked, like yoghurt.
It's like playing Pick Up Sticks.
If you make one wrong move, then.
Your face is round as a bedroom moon.
Don't eat musical notes.
You are a boy in a village of bicycles.
He was a man in a field of cash.
Cut thick slices of the celebration cake.
Drop dead gorgeous.
Drop dead, gorgeous.
What a difference a comma can make.

I Wish February Would Never End

Someone returned your lover,
like a coat that didn't fit.
All day you looked for her in the park.
You said she hurt you while she tried to get sober.
It's ok, you can trust me
like that other guy
you know, the one with the Ph.D.
Let's talk it over:
angel hair, tomatoes, pears, wine.
I'll snap an image with my phone.
Maybe we can make a video.
Saturday nights, the times we'd fall asleep.
She didn't know about you and me.
(Who does she talk to on the scene?)
Change of sheets, someone bled
and that random Facebook post:
"No content," the page said.
That day flew past us, March is dead.
A text was sent, she added up three & three:
(six excuses for celibacy.)
She thought she'd been going crazy till then.
But you were on the brink of her (and me.)
You had to iron out the kinks.

For The Girl Crying on the Steps

When you are loved by one man
in the rain,
in the cold,
in the wee hours of the night,
he won't mind if you come to him
freshly fucked,
recently smoked,
and heavily drunk,
the whiskey spreading rumors
in his mouth.
It's what gets you out of bed in the morning.
There's chow mein congealing in the fridge
but you don't need to be fed.
Your tears are nothing
more than moon dust now.
At the crack of dawn,
you walk the vacant east village streets.
A homeless man is staring at his heroin needle
in Mnemosynic contemplation
as if the piercing of his skin,
the euphoric red rush, will save him.
You know what the need to be saved means.
You're listening to that song, you know, the one
your man played last night.
The cool, fresh watered sidewalk under your heels
washes off your weakness to stay,

not just there, anywhere.
You look into the face of the stranger—
but which?
I'm not going to tell you.
It could be the heroin addict,
the sidewalk washer
or the man you were just with.

Hunky Dory

The cereal I bought this morning was wrong.
I wanted flakes but bought clusters by accident.
The entire morning was wrong, after that.
LifeThyme on Sixth Avenue had this new oat
milk, a probiotic strawberry one
that I wanted for my cereal.
But it wasn't milk, it was thick like yoghurt
so I poured it over fruit.

I wore the wrong jeans.
The ones with the hole in the knee.
Like, I got this hole right here,
but you just can't see it.
This hole in my chest, nobody can fill it.

My horoscope said
I'd get myself into a mess today
that I should just stay in.
I know myself better. I should just shut up.
I don't believe in horror-scopes
but this horrible-scope was right.
I believe in Tarot, go figure.
I am The Emperor, The Star,
The Hierophant and The Moon:
Sun, Moon, Rising, and Venus.

Later, I turned a corner onto West 4th Street
and I ran into you. And your endorphin-fueled
hug hit me like a flashback.
The cereal clusters turned into flakes.
The strawberry yoghurt became milk.
The hole in my jeans was mended.
And nothing else
for the rest of the day went wrong.
But that doesn't matter.

Deadpan

Bony wrist
snapped in two.

You're quiet as a psychopath
as calculating too.

Who won the bread?
No more lines.
Yesterday is dead
after snow got hold

of the polyglot's nose.
Choked on ice
twice as pretty
city to city

tip-toeing in a lab coat
making no sound
needle at the ready.
The hypodermic flow.

Haywire

I had a dream last night:
We headed upstate to L's birthday bash.
It was June. We pulled over
in the nearest gas station to get something to eat.

I changed into my leopard dress
in a concrete bathroom
with blue-ink walls and truck-driver stains.
Brushed my teeth in a stopped-up sink,
copper pennies stuck by gum
underneath. I zipped up my snakeskin boots.

You stole two Frisbees from inside and told me
to run. We peeled out
leaving asphalt millings in our wake.

When I woke, I questioned my need
even in a dream to deem you a thief
when all I wanted to do
was to dress up nicely for you.

Cinema Failure

You're acting like the guy in that movie:
a handyman with a temper and a wrench.
We'll have an award party to celebrate
your favorite show but don't dress
as if you're applying for a loan.
The theatre was here since 1910, the owner
proudly said. As if he owned it since 1910.
He's got a point. He was born above it
lives above it and will probably die above it,
an onlooker said. Don't fear the screech of wheels
down Second Ave. It's an old Chevy Chevette
carrying the noon starlet.
The money isn't really income.
She's too fat and not pretty.
Come back, the director said,
when you're glamorous and skinny.

Nueva Primavera

Take a walk with me in the gold-plated afternoon,
I'm wearing my million-dollar pants.
Let's play hooky in the lime-green grass
lined with lemon trees and sugar bushes.

Forget about refugees, riots and rousts.
Forget about the man with a gun on the A train
unleashing pandemonium
when the train was packed. Or the other man shot
in Tompkins Square Park.

A man in coveralls is crossing the street
carrying a mop and a see-through bag
of paper towels. I stop and I wait,
observing the citrus joy spun from trees.

The light turns green.
I envy you and anyone who can seize
the beauty from the breeze.

Golden Woks

Buy me a pint of rice noodles I'm broke.
The cheap kind for seven dollars
and some odd cents.
The wide kind where the soy sauce clings
to the noodles, succulent to slurp.
I'll eat them so fast I'll get a head rush.
Throw in some vegetable dim sum.
How good does that sound?
This is when I miss Europe most.
5-star meals that sometimes did and did not
impress. And Vienna being so damn cold
with drizzle. I'd veer
off the cobbled lane lined with cafés
to a bookstore in hopes of finding Shakespeare
translated into German. When I did
I memorized sonnets and filled my brain
with rhymes so thick and hearty, poetic fuel
to fuel my gains with friends I'd met
who spoke the language.
We'd drink in other foreign poets,
mostly the Eastern European ones
and what they'd fought for.
Indulge in Linzer Tort
and coffee so good I couldn't stand it.
Wiener Schnitzel when the night was young.
Austrian wine, bread dumplings

and buttered potatoes so creamy
they'd melt on my tongue.
When I was in Bratislava, I bought books
newly released from Slovak poets
who wrote them decades ago
but couldn't tell the world anything
about their struggles before the wall fell.
I don't talk to anyone, anymore.
Not here, not there. I hold my passion in.
I don't like to think about the past.
How things are different now.
I don't want to think about the future, either.
I just want you to buy me a pint of rice noodles,
plain and simple. Succulent and fat.
To fuel me, so I can write.
Can you do that?

My Night Belongs to You

I am here
following you
from room to room
constantly
patiently
listening
to the matter
you place inside
the parenthesis of your affliction.
Endlessly, I hear you
through an orbit of foreign wine
high
like, how
the moon's unsinkable face
belongs nowhere but up.
Questioning
the questionable.
Ribbons
of complaint
slip off your tongue
like a noose that holds no weight.
You're like a lizard.
Lounge. Laze.
Take another pull:
sublime.
Allot space and time

for the urban dusk
to fade.
Say things
that are twisted. Twice.
To mollify.
Wasted words.
Not your words. Mine.
Share the shade.
Pull the covers down.
Come inside.

Lone Wolf

The kind of person you are.
I can think of many lovers.
You can think of many others
but you can't appease me
with wartime-sticks, cumbersome guns
or sly tricks. The desert rises: scorpions lick,
jack rabbits stung. Stolen the sting
from their jump. Cracker crumbs
cake the turf till sunup.
So if you can't catch me by then
where will I be? I'll sink across the ocean
in a plane. Why should I waste time on a slippery
ship? Don't lumber me
among the scotch whiskey crowd:
I am alone
surrounded by dozens of moons and a life
worth ten thousand of you.
Ten countries stroked the backbone of my youth,
the indomitable voices of ten languages to boot.
The bitter reality of the guards. The rifles nudging
the trunk open at the border.
Eastern sun fires, surrenders
to the gate with hot broth caught in my throat
to ratchet up the whole of you
while hiking the Slovak mountainside.
I've never felt

so far from home that very instant
and with violins. America is destined to forget
me and all the names I held on my tongue
like an orange waltz at six.
I danced into my beauty, too
the American affiliate, catering
to the teeth of a shark. Light a cigar
for the lanky girl melting in the grass!
Looming in the ruins of the combat truck.
Nothing but conversations in the noontime-dark
between me and the air in the room.

There is No Brooklyn Bound F Service

no F trains from this station, the sign says
at 42nd street & sixth avenue
(where you spent your day)
to get to the lower east side
you must take the D train downtown
to w 4th street, transfer to the F train
on the upper platform
since this track is express
you must ride back downtown to brooklyn
past delancey street
and switch at jay street metro tech
walk upstairs and back downstairs
to the F train uptown local
past york street
past e bway
to delancey street
on the way home to brooklyn
no F trains running from delancey street
you must take the J train downtown
to fulton street
transfer to the F train downtown local
on the A train platform
listen to the conductor over the intercom
inaudible static
in the heat of subway stations in the confusion of
broken tracks

men work in hard hats
the train is picking up speed
it's the beginning of summer
thank god you took a shower
a woman is talking to herself
a man is jerking off
he's barefoot
may be on drugs
you can't believe ellen doesn't like the beatles
come to think of it, lisa gave up
you wonder what's in your refrigerator
the lady sitting next to you is reading your text
did the mets win?
the ac doesn't work
you can understand why the who
smashed their guitars
what made you suddenly think of that?
god's teaching us a lesson, a man says
to test us, a lady says
to get us to pray, another lady says
jay street metro tech, and thank god
doors open and you rise up finally finally finally
you rise to meet the moon
in all its glorious light

Doorman Building
Brooklyn, New York

The worst thing about living
in a doorman building
is that you have to pass the doorman
every day, even when you're in a shitty mood.
You have to be polite
and say hello, yes it is a great day,
even when it's not
or not say anything at all except thank you
for getting the door
even though you could open doors yourself
since you were a small kid
but you don't want to insult him
by making him think why the hell
he even has his job. He should be used to dealing
with all sorts of people every day, shouldn't he?
It's not as if you're the only person in the world
although more times than not you think you are
and so you picture he'll say to the other doormen:
You know the woman in 5A? Well, she attempts
to open the door herself
as if I don't exist and she's unsociable and bleak
and fakes cheery voices in the morning
when she looks like crap
and she never lets me be a doorman. You'd hope
he'd exonerate you by saying, after all,

she *is* a poet, and you know
how moody *they* can be.
But he doesn't.
You bet doormen gossip.
Like everyone else in every other circle talks.
But you've come a long way
because years ago, when you lived
in a doorman building on York and 81st,
you gave the Monday to Friday doorman
(the 8 – 4 one) 20 extra dollars
in his Christmas tip
because 8 – 4 was a popular time of day
to go places with a toddler
so he opened more doors than you could count,
plus all those packages and all that stuff
he collected, and you decided that year
to give only that doorman more
because he seemed to do more
and that was a mistake
because the other doormen,
the 4 – 12 one and the 12 – 8 one
didn't appreciate not getting that 20 dollar raise.
That is to say they knew and that is to sadly say
you felt like someone out of a Charles Dickens
novel, which goes against everything

you believe in.
Then you suddenly remember
when the whole building was asleep one night,
the scream that tore through the vacant streets
and some guy was looking for someone to mug
and you hurried into the building
when *yours truly* opened the door
and the mugger ran away and you remember
the time before that after you graduated college
and lived in a six-story West Village walkup
and some guy trailed close behind you
as you fumbled with your keys and you screamed
and your packages of cat food cans went flying
and every door unlocked and one neighbor
chased the perpetrator down Morton Street
with a baseball bat
and when the NYPD finally showed up
they yawned and humored you that they'd look
for the guy and you knew they never would or did
because he fled and you fled
under the net of doorman safety.
You're neither proud nor apologetic for your life
(although you feel like a bit of an asshole
 writing this because you elected to live in a
doorman building.)

So when your doorman finally says, You're a poet!
as if he'd taken his last breath, you smile
and you hold your arms up as if under arrest,
and you say, that you can't help it.
You were born that way.

I'm Mad About a Lot of Things Prayer

dear lord i'm mad because the cable's out & i
can't log onto the internet
i'm mad because i can't fit into last year's jeans
i'm mad because my iphone
keeps cutting off stacey
i'm mad because i can't get it right
on e houston street
i'm mad because x blew me off
regarding my coffee message
and i'm mad about x
so i tormented the magic 8 ball
until it said AS I SEE IT
YES

i'm mad about a lot of things
like half-formed rock bands
and how many idiots it took
to fill the white house

i'm mad that someone said
do something constructive with your life!
fuck you i am

i wrote about my painkiller addiction in the
evergreen review

as i walked through the valley
of the shadow of death
i'm mad because america's pharmacies are strict:
how much can one's back really ache?
how many times can one lie about tooth pain?

i'm mad because ellen got mad at me
in paris baguette because i didn't talk s-low-ly
everyone heard
i couldn't shut up about my new found love
for metaphysical poetry
and for myself
and for the stream of consciousness

dear lord i'm mad
please pray for us sinners
from now until the hour of our death
i'll be plagued by first world problems
i'm mad about how spoiled i've become
in the land of the free
in the home of the brave
i'm mad because i'm never wrong
when nothing's good enough
that must be good enough
amen

After a Late Night Jazz Event on the Outskirts of Brooklyn

Let's get lost in a maze of warehouses.
Stumble upon carcasses of Halal carts
and phantom hold-ups
around every corner in my head.
Roam desolate streets we can't find names for.
Sidewalks glisten in sub-zero air.
Taxis don't care.
Legendary neighborhoods are the real deal
before the wrecking ball.
Abandoned shipyards house
zombies drunk with the life of bars and blunts.
Let's steal a Twix, a Coke, a cell phone.
(Ask the night where it keeps its gun.)
Today is one minute young.
Yesterday's music, a web page
my mind hasn't cleared from its cache:
             wired trumpets, the dull thud of bass.
Let the cold wind blow.
The inside of your jacket, warm with you
where I'll rest my head
             is the region I call home.

Bulwark

I hang out, backlit and overcast
in the numbness of your silence.
Let's stew in our assumptions minus
the sky's loud crack knocking
against the moon's teeth.
A blackout. Edible you
dithering on a typewriter in lamplight,
oil-flecked skin, the sweat
of the limelight I cast you in
breaks and spills and seethes.
You can't shake the wreck
crashing from your pen scene after scene.
Unable to swim, the landlubber cracks
one more poem in half, half language,
half-baked. Pronouns incriminate.
Throw shade. Guess who you see?
Not you. Not me.

Catchall

Blowzy, ghetto.
You're all made up
for the wind chime's master.
I'll give you something to regret
when the breezes cease
by the hand of the idiosyncratic
force of seasons.
Decrescendo, eavesdrop.
What made you stop
in your tracks? It's as if you forgot
your lines like a bad actor in a good play.
Time is no longer fat,
time is lanky
hair slicked back.
In fact, dazzling—
not smacked with the bulging eyes
of a bug. Crazy, smug.
You gave up.
Nature's cruelty.
I get that.

Alone

This is a story about a woman in trouble.
What story isn't? This story is also about a man
who came to town, who stole everything
the woman had then traded in that town
for another town and then another
taking this and leaving that.

Yesterday, I blew $6.00 on a can of tomato soup
at Gristedes. I wanted pizza but they charge
$18.00 now with inflation
for the frozen ones and it didn't even have
a cauliflower crust. The discount stores
are no better. Maybe a dollar or two less.
I could drop $4.99 on a slice
at the local pizzeria but if I bought the dough,
the sauce and the cheese
and made my own pie I'd end up spending $21.00
which is too much for one lunch,
just get the slice, I thought
but then if I bought the dough
and the jar of sauce and a package of cheese
I'd have some left over
which would be economical.
I'd save money at the end of the day
but I don't. This is why I'm broke.
And I'm broke because I don't.

So the cycle of spending too little
for just enough adds up to more money spent
in the long run and the cycle spins and spins
like clothes in the washing machine I don't own.
I take my laundry to the local dry cleaner
each week and spend $18.00 for someone else
to do it. My rent went up six hundred bucks
the other month. Just saying.

I watched a movie on Netflix last night
called *Alone*
where this man kidnapped this woman
for no good reason other than he can
and tortured her and this went on
seemingly forever until the big escape scene
that leaves you at the edge of your seat
and the chase scene
and the game of cat and mouse through a forest
and of course the woman tripped
and fell and limped away. But the bad man
found her. And they struggled
on the ground for the knife
or the gun after what seemingly took forever.
She finally got him down again and killed him.
But she couldn't kill him enough.

And isn't it always the case in movies that even
when the bad guy is dead he isn't?
He rises through the pain
and the wounds and here we go
again with the wrestling for the knife or the gun,
at this point what difference
does it make? What stabs and stabs
and won't stop
through all the blood and cuts
until the very, very end and still
even though the woman kept fighting for her life
and finally he was finally really dead
she couldn't kill the bad guy enough.

Dead Ringer

In a dream I follow
a girl home through backlit alleys
over chain-linked fences
across barren lots
       to the Lower East Side.

She's committed a crime.

Frantic, because this time
she's certain she's wounded God.

Her hands in front pockets, eyes on the street.

Her apartment is vacant.
She assembles a fire and nails herself in.
Burning, she rises, as I wake up crying
for her and for what I did.

Good Luck Coffee, or, Why Can't I Find Subject Matter for Poems Like I Used To?

"We have no almond milk today," the girl says.
I think: It's only a steaming drink
in a cardboard mug,
I've got bigger problems than that.
"But lemon cake is half price."
I don't need cake, I need a voice
as heavy as confession.
I won't check my emails without a voice like this
but I'm blessed with succulent lips.
Maybe I should borrow one of Ellen's lovers.
Why not? The words in my verse loved you once
and many others. You (& they)
were published on pages 2 and 4 and 6.
Stanzas 4 and 3 and 2. Back then I was prolific.
It's no wonder when I walk into Starbucks
at 6:30 a.m. I'm half-dead
from a dream-filled night of echoes.

My words luck onto the page
like a good horoscope.
Why does everything I write lately end in hope?

Something Good is Going to Happen Today

A red-bellied bird said, as
it flew up on a windowsill in this big red city,
red as a red room or read as a postcard
on a rainy day.
Something good is going to happen today
and this symbolized hope.

Something good is going to happen today
if you believe it.
I can't tell you what yet
but I'll tell you when it happens, it happens

that the Brooklyn Bridge and the Manhattan
Bridge are close to where I live
but they're not ideal for jumping off.
For one thing, the Manhattan Bridge
has a wire fence on its walkway that you can't
penetrate and the Brooklyn Bridge walkway
expands over traffic. If you're in the mood
to make a splash in water
it won't happen.

Something good is going to happen today.
If I insist, my dentist said,

he's going to have to believe there's something
else going on. There is (isn't) but
I can't stand the sight of non-refulgent weather.
I don't believe in rumors.
I'm not partial to planets when they don't align.

Something good is going to happen today
as I lie in bed at five to midnight,
the minutes are countable stars
and I wonder what it was
that was supposed to happen
as I lie here
with my mind
and my body
and my life.

Who Hasn't

had a love affair with a shooting star
as it explodes over midtown manhattan
squeezing the night into its flexible heat
saxophone song at sunset

who hasn't broken jesus yet

who hasn't weathered a band in a frenzy
of drumbeats
like rainbeats
lovestruck & dumb

in this beautiful city of dirty bliss
you reign high all over the place

it's 5 a.m.
you take what you can get

Gratitude

Many thanks to Linda Kleinbub and her staff at Pink Trees Press, who worked hard to help put this book into the best shape possible. Special thanks to Linda Wulkan for her cover art, to Madeline Artenberg for her attention to detail in proofreading, and to Phillip Giambri for his endless generosity.

About the Author

JENNIFER JUNEAU is a 2025 Acker Award recipient for her poetry. Her short fiction collection *Maze* was published in September 2024 by Roadside Press. She is the author of the full-length poetry collection *More Than Moon,* which was a finalist in the National Poetry Series (Is a Rose Press, 2020), and the novel *ÜberChef USA* (Spork Press, 2019). After living and traveling through Europe for eighteen years, she lives and writes in New York City.

This book is set in Garamond font, a classic serif typeface, tracing its origins to 16th-century France. Designed by Claude Garamond, a French type designer and publisher who is credited with its creation around 1532.